PORTFOLIO OF HAPPINESS

INVESTING IN LIFE, NOT JUST PROPERTY.

AMIT CHOPRA

Made with ♥ on the Notion Press Platform
www.notionpress.com

This book is dedicated to my loving family—the unwavering support that has been my compass through life's unpredictable storms—and to my ever-faithful dog Oliver, whose playful spirit has kept me grounded even on my wildest adventures.

My Family

A special thanks to my mother, Raj Chopra, who poured her heart into my education and nurtured my love for writing—passing on not just her wisdom, but her writing genes. And to my father, Jag Mohan Chopra who never had the chance to read these words, having passed away during COVID—this is for you too.

My Mom and Dad

Contents

Acknowledgements

In July 2021, when the COVID wave was at its peak in India and flights were getting canceled, I found myself stranded in uncertainty and grief, having just lost my dad. Amid the chaos at Meta and a critical crossroads in my career—with offers from both Microsoft and Amazon—my wife became my personal helpline.

With a blend of humor and wisdom, she simply said, "You've already done Google, Facebook, and Microsoft. Why not Amazon?"

That moment, as bittersweet as it was, set me on a new, unexpected path. It was during this turbulent time that I promised, albeit in a passing remark, to someday write a book—a promise that, thanks to life's surprises (including a unexpected layoff from Microsoft), has finally taken shape in these pages.

I owe this journey to my incredible wife, who gracefully managed work and home during my countless trips, and to my devoted dog Oliver, who learned to master the art of solitude while I was away. Thank you, dear family, for making every step of this adventure possible and inspiring me to embrace a life rich in meaning and laughter.

Foreword

During a recent reunion with my high school friends, fellow mid-fifties achievers with stable careers, well-settled families, and hard-won financial success—I was struck by a surprising blend of admiration and quiet envy.

As we exchanged stories over drinks and dinner, exclusively catered for our group, I recounted my adventures mentoring college students and traveling to remote corners of the world on my own dime. While they celebrated the comforts and security their wealth afforded, many of them admitted, almost wistfully, that something was missing—a spark of purpose that money alone couldn't buy.

In our candid conversations, it became clear that the true measure of wealth isn't found in the balance of a bank account or the number of property investments, but in the impact we make and the richness of the experiences we create. My friends confessed that while they reveled in the pleasures that material success brings, they couldn't help but wonder if there was more to life than the relentless pursuit of accumulation.

They saw in my journey a chance to break free from the predictable rhythm of comfort and routine—a life where fulfillment is derived from meaningful connections and moments that truly matter.

"This book is an invitation—a call to reconsider and redefine what wealth really means."

I challenge you to question the old narratives that tie success solely to financial gain. Instead, imagine a life where you invest as much in experiences, relationships, and personal growth as you do in assets. It's time to shift from a life of mere consumption to one of conscious creation, where every moment is an opportunity to leave a legacy of joy, impact, and authenticity.

Let's embark on this journey together, and explore the true rewards of a life lived fully, beyond the confines of conventional wealth.

Preface

Every journey begins with a single step, and the steps we choose often define our lives far more than we imagine. This book was born from my own quest for a richer, more meaningful life—a quest that took shape after decades spent navigating the demanding world of technology. I built my career at companies like Microsoft, Google, Meta, and Amazon, and by conventional measures, I had "made it." Yet, amidst the intensity of high-stakes business, I felt an unsettling emptiness, a sense that something essential was missing. The relentless pursuit of more—more wealth, more status, more validation—led me to question what I was truly investing my time in.

This book is not a memoir of my professional achievements. Instead, it's a reflective exploration of the stark realities that often lie beneath our modern obsession with accumulation. It's about the paradox of having everything on paper, yet feeling incomplete in the spaces between. I invite you to join me as we examine long-held beliefs about success and explore the untapped potential of investing in experiences, nurturing our well-being, and forging deep, lasting connections. Whether you're already on this path or just beginning to sense that there's more to life than the next big deal, I hope these pages inspire you to look beyond the obvious and embark on your own journey towards true fulfillment.

Prologue

A Personal Awakening: From Achievement to Impact

For three decades, I navigated the high-stakes corridors of the corporate world, working with industry giants like Microsoft, Google, Meta, and Amazon. I experienced the allure of success firsthand: the prestige, the security, and the validation of a well-padded resume. But beneath the surface, a fundamental question began to emerge: What am I truly gaining?

My path took an unexpected turn when I stepped away from that high-pressure environment, moving beyond stock performance and boardroom battles, towards something less tangible yet infinitely more rewarding: impact and purpose. I shifted my focus from conference calls to conversations with students, from KPIs to knowledge-sharing, and began to design a life centered around giving back.

My calendar now revolves around journeys, many of which include visits to local universities where I offer guest lectures. I share lessons from my years at the forefront of technology, insights into navigating a rapidly changing world, and the realities of success beyond paychecks and promotions. The response is deeply gratifying. Students gain confidence in their ambitions, and faculty appreciate new perspectives on integrating career aspirations with a fulfilling life.

The most common question I receive is, "Why don't you charge for this?" It's often assumed that only immense wealth could enable such generosity. The truth is different. While I have financial stability, my most valuable asset is not money. It's the ability to make a difference. The fulfillment I derive from each lecture, each mentoring session, each conversation that helps shape a young mind, far surpasses any monetary reward. This is a different kind of wealth, measured not in currency but in impact, in lives touched, and in a community enriched.

This journey has reinforced a powerful and transformative lesson: True wealth isn't about accumulating for an abstract future; it's about investing in the present and in the well-being of others. It's about recognizing that we all have the power to redefine what a meaningful life looks like. It's about choosing to invest in experiences, in people, and in the moments that truly matter. Because, ultimately, the happiness we cultivate in others often returns to us in ways that transcend traditional measures of success.

CHAPTER ONE

The Illusion of Traditional Wealth and Success

From an early age, we are fed a formula for success: Study hard, get a well-paying job, climb the corporate ladder, and secure your future. The ultimate dream? Retire wealthy and finally start enjoying life. But what if this entire framework is flawed? What if we've been sold a version of success that serves corporations more than it serves us?

This chapter will explore how society's traditional model of wealth accumulation has evolved, the ingrained beliefs about money and success, and why these notions often lead to a sense of emptiness despite material achievements. It will also examine the historical and cultural roots of these beliefs, particularly in the Indian context, and how they continue to shape our perceptions.

Historical and Cultural Roots: The Legacy of the 'Babu' and Middle-Class Mentality

India's modern economic landscape is built on enduring lessons from history, where the seeds of financial caution were sown long ago. During the British colonial era, the archetype of the 'babu' emerged—a figure marked by bureaucratic rigidity, an unyielding fear of risk, and a steadfast commitment to protocol. This persona was not merely a professional role; it was a way of life that instilled in the Indian middle class a deep respect for order and frugality.

Imagine an aged Mumbai bungalow with faded colonial architecture and weathered verandas. Here, family gatherings are a ritual, and the stories told by elders are as much about survival as they are about success. Uncle Ramesh, a retired government clerk with deep-set wrinkles that speak of decades spent in service, sits in his favorite armchair. With a gentle smile and eyes that have seen both hardship and triumph, he recounts tales of his youth. He describes, in vivid detail, how even the smallest error in his meticulous accounts at the office could provoke a stern reprimand from his superiors—a lesson that ingrained in him the belief that every rupee was sacrosanct. His anecdotes, filled with both humor and gravity, illustrate a time when money was a lifeline, and every expense had to be justified with an almost religious fervor.

The cautious mindset of the babu is more than a relic of colonial bureaucracy; it has become the very DNA of financial behavior in many Indian families. This inherited prudence, passed down like a treasured heirloom, shaped a generation that valued security over spontaneity. In that same old bungalow, conversations often turn to the merits of saving versus spending. It is common to hear, "We must never squander what our forefathers struggled so hard to earn." This conviction, born of years marked by uncertainty, continues to inform decisions even in an era of apparent abundance.

In the aftermath of independence, India faced economic hardships that left an indelible mark on the national psyche. Food shortages, infrastructural challenges, and a pervasive sense of scarcity meant that every rupee was viewed as a safeguard against an unpredictable future. I recall, with both nostalgia and a touch of melancholy, the stories my parents shared about their youth. Every small victory in managing the household budget was celebrated as if it were a triumph over fate itself.

Consider Aarav, a young professional whose life was still haunted by the stories of rationing and long lines for basic goods. Despite achieving financial stability as an adult, Aarav found himself hesitant to invest in experiences that might provide fleeting pleasure—a spontaneous trip, a weekend outing, or even a simple family dinner at a restaurant. **The mantra, "Save today for a secure tomorrow," was not just parental advice; it was an ethos that defined his very approach to life.**

This deep-seated caution explains why even those who have transcended modest beginnings often default to conservative spending habits. For many, wealth is less a means to an end than it is an ever-present reminder of the precariousness of life.

The scars of past financial crises have left many with a lingering mistrust of modern institutions. Witnessing instances of bureaucratic corruption or experiencing personal financial setbacks have instilled a belief that money is best safeguarded in tangible forms. In many families, the idea of investing in abstract instruments like stocks or bonds feels too uncertain—a gamble with one's hard-earned savings.

Take Meera's story, for example. Growing up, she was regaled with accounts of relatives who lost their life savings in poorly managed bank schemes during the tumultuous economic liberalizations of the 1990s. This legacy of caution led her family to invest predominantly in real estate—a piece of land or a well-located apartment that could be seen, touched, and understood. For them, such investments were not just financial decisions; they were a form of tangible security in an uncertain world.

The Illusion of the Traditional Path: An Endless Chase?

Consider Ananya, a brilliant software engineer who followed the conventional path to the letter. She studied at a prestigious university, landed a six-figure job at a top tech company, and worked tirelessly for years, aiming for that elusive promotion. Her parents beamed with pride, and her LinkedIn profile was the envy of her peers. She had done everything "right."

Yet deep inside, Ananya felt a growing void. Her days blurred into endless meetings, her social life revolved around networking events, and she could barely recall the last time she had a spontaneous moment of joy. The higher she climbed, the more pressure she felt to keep climbing. She could now afford five-star vacations, but when she finally took time off, she spent the entire trip checking emails and feeling guilty for not being productive.

Then, one day, an old college friend visited her from Seattle. He had taken a different path—choosing to work less, travel more, and prioritize relationships over promotions. Over dinner, as they caught up, Ananya was struck by how relaxed and genuinely happy he seemed. She, on the other hand, was constantly anxious, worried about deadlines, performance reviews, and whether she was "falling behind." That night, she lay awake, replaying their conversation. For the first time, she wondered—was she really successful, or was she just playing a game designed by someone else?

The Neuroscience of Discontent

Recent studies in positive psychology reveal a paradox: Beyond a basic income threshold (approximately $75,000 annually in the U.S., as per Princeton University's 2010 study), increased wealth has diminishing returns on happiness. Yet, societal narratives keep us chasing higher salaries, mistaking momentary dopamine spikes from purchases for lasting fulfillment.

Ananya, the software engineer who followed the "right" path. Her story mirrors findings from the World Happiness Report, which emphasizes social support and personal freedom as stronger predictors of life satisfaction than GDP. When Ananya's Seattle friend shared his joy in prioritizing travel and relationships, her anxiety wasn't just existential—it was biological. Chronic stress from relentless achievement triggers cortisol spikes, eroding mental and physical health.

The Pitfalls of Traditional Success: A Deeper Examination

Society glorifies wealth but often fails to acknowledge the cost of acquiring it. It rarely talks about the mental exhaustion, the missed birthdays, the emotional toll of high-pressure careers, and the gnawing feeling of "Is this it?" We celebrate billionaires but don't ask whether they're happy. We measure success in salaries and titles but ignore metrics like mental peace, personal growth, and genuine human connection. This obsession with traditional success metrics often leads to a dangerous trap: lifestyle inflation.

As people earn more, they spend more—bigger homes, fancier cars, expensive vacations—all in an attempt to "keep up." But this cycle rarely brings lasting satisfaction. Instead, it creates a treadmill effect, where no matter how much one earns, it never feels like enough.

Take the example of Vikram, a senior executive at a Fortune 500 company. He once lived a simple, content life. But as his salary increased, so did his expenses—his home got bigger, his vacations more extravagant, his children's schooling more elite. At first, it felt like progress. But soon, he realized that with every upgrade came new pressures—higher mortgage payments, steeper expectations at work, and a constant fear of losing the lifestyle he had built. He was wealthier than ever, yet felt more trapped than he had in his early career.

Moreover, the pursuit of traditional success can strain relationships and erode our sense of self. The long hours, the constant pressure to achieve, and the focus on external validation can leave us feeling disconnected from our loved ones and ourselves. We may find ourselves sacrificing our values, our passions, and our well-being in the pursuit of a goal that, in the end, does not bring us true happiness.

Moving Beyond the Illusion: A Call for Redefinition

Let's challenge the conventional wisdom about success and wealth. What if we questioned societal norms and redefined what a successful life truly looks like? What if it were about designing a life where happiness isn't postponed but lived in the present, rather than accumulating wealth for a future that may never come?

The challenge for modern individuals is to reconcile the legacy of prudent financial management with a growing awareness of the need to truly live, to embrace experiences that enrich life in ways that mere numbers on a balance sheet never can. It is about integrating mindfulness and emotional fulfillment into a framework that has long been dominated by caution and conservatism. It's about breaking free from the illusion that more money and more status will automatically lead to more happiness.

The choice, ultimately, is ours. Because real success isn't about climbing the highest mountain—it's about making sure the view is worth it once you get there. It's about designing a life that aligns with our values, nourishes our soul, and allows us to make a meaningful contribution to the world.

Action Plan:

1. Write your personal definition of success (include non-material elements like relationships or creativity).
2. Track daily activities for one week—note which ones align with your definition vs. societal expectations.

Reflection Questions:

1. What societal "script" have you followed without questioning?
2. How would your life change if you prioritized joy over approval?

THE INDIAN UPPER MIDDLE CLASS: REDEFINING HAPPINESS.

India's upper-middle class stands at a fascinating crossroads. This dynamic and rapidly evolving segment of society, a key driver of the nation's economic, social, and cultural transformation, is not only shaping India's future but also playing a crucial role in redefining the very meaning of happiness and success in an increasingly globalized yet deeply traditional context. This chapter explores how this influential group's aspirations, challenges, and evolving values relate to the core concept of building a "Portfolio of Happiness."

Defining the Indian Upper Middle Class

The Indian upper-middle class is a diverse group, defined by a combination of factors:

- **Economic Indicators:** Stable, relatively high incomes, enabling comfortable lifestyles, property ownership, and access to quality education and healthcare.
- **Educational Attainment:** Advanced degrees and employment in white-collar professions (technology, management, finance, medicine).
- **Social Capital:** Strong social networks, both within India and globally, facilitating professional and personal advancement.
- **Cultural Exposure:** Greater exposure to global trends, lifestyles, and values through travel, international media, and education.

This group's experiences and choices are particularly relevant to the "Portfolio of Happiness" because they highlight the complexities of pursuing well-being in a world that often equates success with material wealth.

Redefining Success and Happiness: A Portfolio Perspective

The Indian upper-middle class is redefining success and happiness in ways that resonate strongly with the "Portfolio of Happiness" concept:

- **Embracing a Broader Definition of Wealth:** They are moving beyond material wealth to value experiences, relationships, personal growth, and social impact—all key components of a diversified "Portfolio of Happiness."
- **Seeking Purposeful Careers:** The shift towards careers that align with values and contribute to society reflects the importance of purpose and meaning in a fulfilling life.
- **Prioritizing Well-being:** The focus on physical and mental health underscores the fundamental role of well-being in overall happiness.
- **Fostering Inclusive Values:** The embrace of progressive values aligns with the desire for a just and equitable society, contributing to a broader sense of collective happiness.
- **Driving Social Change:** Their role in driving social change reflects a recognition that individual happiness is intertwined with the well-being of the community.

The Indian upper-middle class offers a compelling case study in how a dynamic and influential group navigates the complexities of pursuing happiness in a rapidly changing world. Their journey, marked by a desire to balance tradition and modernity, material success and personal fulfillment, highlights the importance of constructing a diversified "Portfolio of Happiness." Their evolving values and priorities provide valuable insights into how societies can move towards a more holistic and sustainable understanding of well-being, one that recognizes the interconnectedness of individual, social, and economic factors in the pursuit of a truly fulfilling life.

Action Plan:

1. Audit your "happiness portfolio": List experiences, relationships, and possessions. Which category dominates?
2. Plan one low-cost experience (e.g., a family storytelling night) to prioritize connection.

Reflection Questions:

1. Which cultural values (e.g., frugality, stability) do you want to keep or redefine?
2. How does your career align with your inner values?

CHAPTER THREE

Overcoming Cultural Barriers

India is a land of rich cultural heritage and deep-rooted traditions. While these traditions offer a sense of identity and belonging, they can sometimes create barriers to adopting new perspectives and embracing change. This chapter explores some of the cultural barriers that may hinder the shift towards a more experience-driven approach to life and offers strategies for overcoming them.

One of the main barriers is the emphasis on conformity and social expectations. Indian society often places a high value on fulfilling one's duties and obligations, both to family and community. This can lead individuals to prioritize stability and security over personal fulfillment and exploration.

For example, young people may feel pressured to choose a career path that is deemed respectable by their families, even if it doesn't align with their passions or talents. They may also feel obligated to prioritize marriage and family life over pursuing their individual dreams and aspirations.

Another barrier is the fear of failure and the stigma associated with taking risks. Indian culture often views failure as a sign of weakness or incompetence, which can discourage individuals from stepping outside their comfort zones and pursuing unconventional paths. This fear can be particularly strong in the context of career choices and financial decisions, where the pressure to succeed is high.

Additionally, the concept of karma can sometimes be misinterpreted as a justification for accepting one's circumstances without striving for change. While the original intention of karma is to emphasize personal responsibility and the consequences of one's actions, it can sometimes be used to rationalize inaction and a sense of helplessness.

So how do we overcome these cultural barriers and create a more open and accepting environment for pursuing a meaningful and experience-rich life? Here are some strategies:

- **Promote Open Dialogue and Awareness:** Encourage conversations about alternative perspectives on success and happiness. Share stories of individuals who have broken free from traditional norms and found fulfillment in unconventional ways.
- **Challenge Limiting Beliefs:** Question the assumptions and beliefs that hold you back from pursuing your dreams. Are these beliefs truly your own, or are they inherited from your family or society?
- **Embrace a Growth Mindset:** View failures and setbacks as opportunities for learning and growth. Cultivate resilience and the willingness to experiment and take calculated risks. In Japan, the concept of "ikigai" (reason

for being) emphasizes purpose over perfection.

- **Redefine Success on Your Own Terms:** Don't let society dictate what success means to you. Define your own values and create your own personal definition of a life well-lived.
- **Seek out Supportive Communities:** Surround yourself with people who share your values and aspirations. Find communities, both online and offline, that celebrate individuality, creativity, and personal growth.
- **Lead by Example:** Be a role model for others by living your life authentically and pursuing your passions with courage and conviction. Your actions can inspire others to break free from limiting beliefs and pursue their own dreams.
- **Celebrate Individuality and Diversity:** Recognize and celebrate the unique talents and perspectives of each individual. Embrace diversity in all its forms and create a society where everyone feels empowered to live their truth.

Indian families often equate non-traditional careers with rebellion. Riya, a 28-year-old from Jaipur, faced resistance when she left her engineering job to start a organic farm. She bridged the gap by hosting monthly family dinners where she explained how her work aligned with values of sustainability (a concept rooted in Ayurveda). Over time, her parents became her biggest supporters.

Overcoming cultural barriers is not an easy task, but it is essential for creating a society where individuals feel empowered to pursue their dreams and live a life of purpose and joy. It requires a collective effort to challenge limiting beliefs, promote open dialogue, and celebrate the diversity of human experience.

Action Plan:

1. Challenge one limiting belief this week (e.g., "Risk-taking is reckless").
2. Join a community (online/offline) that supports unconventional goals (e.g., creative writing groups).

Reflection Questions:

1. What belief have you inherited that no longer serves you?
2. Who in your life would support your authentic path?

CHAPTER FOUR

The Duality of Wealth: Redefining Success Beyond Accumulation

For decades, society has programmed us to measure wealth in numbers—bank balances, real estate holdings, and stock portfolios. The bigger the number, the more successful you are. The logic is simple: money equals security, and security equals happiness. But what if we've been measuring wealth the wrong way? What if real wealth isn't just about financial security but something far more profound—freedom, relationships, experiences, and peace of mind?

Consider the story of Rajesh, a 50-year-old executive at a global consulting firm. On paper, Rajesh had it all—an enviable salary, multiple properties, luxury cars, and a network of high-powered friends. He was the embodiment of conventional success. But the cracks in his carefully curated world began to show when he suffered a mild heart attack. As he lay in the hospital, surrounded by beeping machines and sterile walls, Rajesh had an unsettling realization: despite his material success, he felt completely alone. His workaholic lifestyle had cost him his health, distanced him from his children, and turned his marriage into little more than a transactional partnership.

For years, he had justified the long hours, missed vacations, and postponed family time as necessary sacrifices for a better future. Yet here he was, his body rebelling against the very lifestyle he had worked so hard to build. When his doctor asked him about his stress levels, Rajesh laughed bitterly. Stress had become his way of life. His success, once a source of pride, now felt like a burden—one that had stolen years of his life that he could never get back.

Rajesh's story is not unique. Across the world, millions chase financial security without questioning what that security is meant to buy them. A high salary, a big house, and a luxury car are often symbols of success, but they don't automatically translate to a fulfilled life. True wealth, as Rajesh painfully learned, isn't just about what you accumulate—it's about what you cultivate.

Real wealth is the ability to choose how you spend your time. It's the freedom to wake up in the morning and not feel trapped by obligations that don't serve you. It's the richness of deep, meaningful relationships—the kind where you can call a friend in the middle of the night and know they'll pick up. It's about experiences—watching a sunrise on a secluded beach, traveling with your children while they still want to hold your hand, sharing a meal with your aging parents while they still remember your childhood stories.

However, in the relentless pursuit of more, even those who have seemingly achieved financial abundance can fall prey to the lure of constant accumulation. Family gatherings and friendly reunions, once filled with warmth and shared laughter, can quickly turn into arenas for quiet rivalries, where discussions about property and profit replace genuine connection. The very bonds that should nurture our spirits become strained when the promise of one more asset eclipses the value of togetherness.

Consider a family where every decision is weighed in terms of inheritance or property share—a situation where the drive for financial security transforms into an unspoken competition, fracturing relationships that have weathered life's ups and downs. Even among the wealthy, the idea of leaving behind an even larger legacy can lead to conflicts, overshadowing the deeper, intangible wealth of trust, love, and mutual respect. Such divisions remind us that the pursuit of material gain often comes at a steep personal cost. When the chase for more creates rifts between hearts, the true measure of wealth—our connections and shared experiences—gets lost in the balance sheets of our lives.

This chapter explores the idea that real wealth isn't found in spreadsheets but in moments. It discusses why traditional definitions of wealth often leave people feeling empty and how shifting our perspective can lead to a richer, more meaningful life. It also examines the potential downsides of pursuing wealth at the expense of relationships and personal well-being. **Because at the end of the day, wealth isn't just about accumulating—it's about living.**

True wealth is measured by the freedom to love, laugh, and live fully. Embrace experiences that enrich your soul over possessions that weigh you down. True abundance isn't measured by the assets you own, but by the bonds you cherish. Let not the pursuit of more drive a wedge between hearts, for unity is the richest legacy of all.

Action Plan:

1. Conduct a "wealth audit": List 5 non-material assets (e.g., trusted friendships, hobbies).
2. Replace one material purchase this month with an experience (e.g., a picnic vs. new shoes).

Reflection Questions:

1. When have you felt "rich" without spending money?
2. What legacy do you want to leave—assets or memories?

CHAPTER FIVE

LIVING WITH ZERO REGRETS: LESSONS FROM "DIE WITH ZERO"

We live in a world that constantly tells us to save for the future. From a young age, we are taught to defer gratification, to work hard and accumulate wealth so that one day, we can finally enjoy the fruits of our labor. But what if that "one day" never comes? What if we spend our lives preparing for a future that may never arrive, only to look back with regret on a life unlived?

"Die With Zero: Getting the Most Out of Your Money and Your Life" by Bill Perkins challenges this conventional wisdom. It argues that our goal should not be to simply accumulate wealth, but to maximize our lifetime fulfillment. It's not about having the most money when you die, but about having the most meaningful experiences throughout your life. The book's principles resonate deeply with the core philosophy of redefining wealth and designing a life of purpose, and offer a valuable framework for individuals seeking to optimize their well-being.

Time is Our Most Valuable Resource

The central idea in "Die With Zero" is that time is our most precious resource. Unlike money, which can be earned and accumulated, time is finite and irreplaceable. Every day that we postpone joy, every experience we delay, is a day we can never get back. As Perkins writes, "Life is measured in time, not money."

This concept challenges the traditional approach to financial planning, which often prioritizes maximizing wealth at the expense of living fully in the present. It encourages us to shift our focus from how much money we can accumulate to how we can best utilize our time to create lasting memories and enrich our lives.

This principle is particularly relevant in the Indian context, where there is often a strong emphasis on saving for the future and fulfilling familial responsibilities. While financial security is undoubtedly important, it's equally crucial to recognize that life is happening now. We must find a balance between planning for tomorrow and living for today.

Prioritizing Experiences

"Die With Zero" advocates for prioritizing experiences over material possessions. The book argues that the value of an experience is not just the enjoyment we derive from it in the moment, but also the memories and stories we create, which can enrich our lives for years to come.

Think about a time when you had a truly memorable experience - a trip, a concert, a meaningful conversation with a loved one. How did that experience make you feel? How did it shape your perspective or create a lasting memory?

Experiences have a unique power to enhance our well-being. They can strengthen our relationships, expand our horizons, and provide us with a sense of purpose and fulfillment. They are the building blocks of a rich and meaningful life.

In the Indian context, this could mean making a conscious effort to incorporate more experiential elements into our lives. Instead of always opting for the safest, most conservative financial choices, we might allocate resources for experiences that align with our values and bring us joy. This could involve anything from traveling to explore India's diverse landscapes and cultural heritage to pursuing a passion like music or dance, or simply spending more quality time with family and friends.

Optimizing for Lifetime Fulfillment

"Die With Zero" introduces the concept of optimizing for lifetime fulfillment, which involves making conscious decisions about how to spend our time and money at different stages of life to maximize our overall well-being.

The book suggests that there are certain experiences that are best enjoyed at specific ages. For example, traveling and adventure might be more appealing and fulfilling in our youth when we have more energy and fewer responsibilities. Spending time with young children is most rewarding when they are still young and impressionable.

By being intentional about when we have certain experiences, we can ensure that we are getting the most out of them. This approach contrasts with the traditional model of postponing enjoyment until retirement, which may result in missing out on experiences that would have been more meaningful at an earlier age.

In the Indian context, this could involve a shift in perspective on life planning. While traditional milestones like marriage, children, and career advancement remain important, there could be more emphasis on front-loading experiences and prioritizing personal fulfillment at every stage of life.

Breaking Free from the Accumulation Trap

"Die With Zero" challenges the idea that we should always be striving to accumulate more money. The book argues that beyond a certain point, additional wealth does not necessarily translate to increased happiness or fulfillment. In fact, it can sometimes lead to increased stress, anxiety, and a sense of being trapped in a never-ending cycle of working and spending.

The book encourages us to question our motivations for accumulating wealth. Are we pursuing money for the sake of security, or are we chasing an illusion of happiness and fulfillment? By understanding our true motivations, we can make more conscious choices about how to allocate our resources and prioritize what truly matters.

This concept is particularly relevant in today's consumer-driven society, where we are constantly bombarded with messages that equate happiness with material possessions. It encourages us to cultivate a mindset of contentment and to find joy in experiences, relationships, and personal growth, rather than constantly striving for more.

Designing a Life of Purpose and Joy

The lessons of "Die With Zero" provide a powerful framework for designing a life of purpose and joy. By recognizing the value of time, prioritizing experiences, optimizing for lifetime fulfillment, and breaking free from the accumulation trap, we can create a life that is rich in meaning, connection, and joy.

This approach aligns with the principles of redefining wealth, emphasizing that true wealth is not measured in money but in the quality of our experiences, the strength of our relationships, and the depth of our personal fulfillment. It encourages us to move beyond the traditional model of success, which often prioritizes financial achievement at the expense of well-being, and to embrace a more holistic vision of a life well-lived.

Action Plan:

1. List 3 experiences you've postponed (e.g., a trip, learning a skill). Schedule one within 6 months.
2. Calculate your "time budget": How many hours/week are spent on joy vs. obligation?

Reflection Questions:

1. What would you regret not doing if life ended tomorrow?
2. How does delaying joy rob you of fulfillment?

CHAPTER SIX

BUILDING A MEANINGFUL AND FINANCIALLY SUSTAINABLE LIFE

In the pursuit of a life well-lived, the question often arises: How do we reconcile our desire for purpose and meaning with the practicalities of financial security? How do we design a life that is both deeply fulfilling and sustainable in the long run? This chapter bridges these two crucial aspects, offering a comprehensive guide to building a life that is both meaningful and financially sound, particularly within the Indian context.

I. Defining Meaning in the Indian Context

India, with its rich tapestry of traditions, philosophies, and spiritual practices, offers a unique perspective on the concept of meaning. For centuries, concepts like dharma (one's duty), seva (selfless service), and moksha (liberation) have shaped the understanding of a purposeful life. In contemporary India, while these traditional values remain relevant, they are often interwoven with modern aspirations for personal growth, social impact, and creative expression.

- **Dharma and Purpose:** Dharma, often translated as "duty," goes beyond mere obligation. It encompasses one's unique purpose and role in life, aligned with their inherent talents and values. In today's context, this could translate to finding work that not only provides financial stability but also allows you to contribute your unique skills and passions to the world.
- **Seva and Contribution:** The spirit of seva, or selfless service, is deeply ingrained in Indian culture. It emphasizes the importance of giving back to society and contributing to the well-being of others. This could involve volunteering your time, supporting a cause you believe in, or using your professional skills to make a positive impact.
- **Moksha and Self-Realization:** While moksha refers to spiritual liberation, its essence—the pursuit of self-realization and inner peace—is highly relevant to the modern quest for meaning. It encourages us to look beyond external achievements and cultivate a sense of inner fulfillment through practices like mindfulness, self-reflection, and creative expression.

II. Strategies for Building a Meaningful Life

Building a meaningful life is not a one-size-fits-all endeavor. It requires introspection, experimentation, and a willingness to step outside your comfort zone. Here are some strategies, tailored to the Indian context, to guide you on this journey:

- **Identify Your Core Values:** What truly matters to you? Is it family, creativity, social impact, knowledge, spirituality, or something else? Understanding your core values is the foundation for making meaningful choices in all areas of your life.
- **Align Your Work with Your Values:** Seek work that not only provides financial security but also allows you to express your values and contribute to something you believe in. This could involve finding a purpose-driven company, starting your own social enterprise, or using your skills to volunteer for a cause you care about.
- **Cultivate Meaningful Relationships:** Invest time and energy in building strong, supportive relationships with family, friends, and community members. Nurture these connections through open communication, shared experiences, and mutual support.
- **Embrace Lifelong Learning:** In India's rapidly evolving landscape, continuous learning is essential for both personal and professional growth. Pursue knowledge and skills that align with your interests and passions, whether it's through formal education, online courses, or self-directed learning.
- **Practice Mindfulness and Self-Reflection:** Cultivate a deeper connection with yourself through practices like

meditation, yoga, or journaling. These practices can help you gain clarity about your values, manage stress, and make more conscious choices.

- **Engage in Creative Expression:** Whether it's through art, music, writing, or any other form of creative expression, find outlets to express your unique talents and perspectives. Creativity can be a powerful source of joy, self-discovery, and meaning.
- **Contribute to Society:** Find ways to give back to your community and contribute to the greater good. This could involve volunteering your time, supporting a social cause, or using your skills to address social challenges.

III. *Financial Strategies for Experiential Wealth*

While meaning is paramount, financial stability is also crucial for long-term well-being and for enabling the pursuit of meaningful experiences. However, traditional Indian approaches to financial planning, often centered around risk aversion and long-term savings, may need to be adapted to prioritize experiential wealth.

Here are some strategies:

1. **Shift Your Mindset from Saving to Investing in Experiences:** Instead of solely focusing on accumulating wealth for the distant future, allocate a portion of your resources to creating meaningful experiences in the present. This could involve travel, cultural events, learning new skills, or pursuing hobbies that bring you joy.

2. **Create a Financial Plan that Balances Security and Experiences:** Work with a financial advisor to create a plan that meets your long-term financial goals while also allowing you to invest in experiences that enrich your life. This plan should consider your income, expenses, risk tolerance, and time horizon.

3. **Prioritize Experiences that Align with Your Values:** When choosing how to spend your money on experiences, prioritize those that align with your core values and contribute to your personal growth. For example, if you value family and connection, prioritize experiences that bring you closer to your loved ones.

4. **Leverage Technology and Innovation:** Explore how technology can help you optimize your finances and access unique experiences. This could involve using budgeting apps, investing in experiential travel platforms, or participating in online communities that share your interests.

5. **Embrace Conscious Consumption:** Be mindful of your spending habits and avoid unnecessary purchases that don't add lasting value to your life. Instead, focus on investing in experiences and relationships that create lasting memories and contribute to your overall well-being.

6. **Build Multiple Income Streams:** In today's dynamic economy, relying solely on a single source of income can be risky. Explore opportunities to diversify your income streams through side hustles, investments, or entrepreneurial ventures. This can provide greater financial security and free up resources for pursuing meaningful experiences.

IV. Balancing Meaning and Money

Aparna's Journey: Aparna, a successful software engineer, felt a growing disconnect between her high-paying job and her passion for environmental conservation. She began volunteering for a local NGO on weekends, using her technical skills to develop their website and manage their online campaigns. Over time, she realized she wanted to dedicate her full time to this cause.

Aparna took a calculated risk, transitioning to a lower-paying role at the NGO while supplementing her income with freelance projects. She also made conscious spending choices, prioritizing experiences like attending sustainability conferences and volunteering in ecological restoration projects. While her income decreased, Aparna's sense of purpose and fulfillment soared. She found deep meaning in her work, built strong relationships with like-minded individuals, and felt more aligned with her values than ever before.

Rahul's Reinvention: Rahul, a middle-aged banker, had a stable career and a comfortable lifestyle. However, he felt a nagging sense of unfulfillment. He had always dreamed of being a writer but had never pursued it seriously. With the support of his family, Rahul decided to take a sabbatical from his banking job to write a novel.

Rahul used his savings to fund his sabbatical, carefully budgeting his expenses and seeking out affordable writing retreats. He also leveraged his financial expertise to offer workshops and online courses on personal finance for writers, creating an additional income stream. The experience of writing his novel was transformative. He discovered a hidden talent, connected with a community of fellow writers, and found a new sense of meaning and purpose.

A Holistic Approach to Life

Building a meaningful and financially sustainable life is not about choosing one over the other. It's about finding a harmonious balance between purpose and prosperity, aligning your actions with your values, and making conscious choices about how you allocate your time, energy, and resources.

In the Indian context, this involves integrating traditional wisdom with modern aspirations, honoring our cultural heritage while embracing new possibilities, and contributing to a society that values both individual fulfillment and collective well-being.

By following these strategies and drawing inspiration from the experiences of others, you can create a life that is not only abundant in material wealth but also rich in meaning, connection, and joy.

Action Plan:

1. Align one work task with your values this week (e.g., mentoring a junior colleague).
2. Explore a side hustle or volunteer opportunity that blends skills and passion.

Reflection Questions:

1. How does your current work serve others or your community?
2. What fear holds you back from pursuing a purpose-driven path?

CHAPTER SEVEN

FROM KNOWING TO LIVING: BRIDGING THE GAP BETWEEN WISDOM AND ACTION

We've all had those moments of profound clarity, those flashes of insight where a truth becomes undeniably obvious. It might be the realization that we need to prioritize our health, nurture our relationships, or pursue a passion we've long neglected. In these moments, we see the path forward with perfect clarity. We know what we need to do.

Yet, how often does this knowing translate into doing? How often do we find ourselves stuck in the gap between intellectual understanding and tangible action? This is the paradox of obvious wisdom—the frustrating reality that even when we know what's best for us, we struggle to implement that knowledge in our lives. This chapter delves into this paradox, explores the reasons behind our inaction, and provides strategies for bridging the gap between knowing and living.

The Paradox of Obvious Wisdom: Why We Don't Do What We Know

The human experience is rife with examples of this paradox. We know that regular exercise is crucial for our physical and mental well-being, yet we find ourselves making excuses to skip the gym. We know that spending quality time with loved ones strengthens our bonds, yet we get caught up in the whirlwind of work and other commitments. We know that pursuing our passions brings us joy and fulfillment, yet we allow fear and self-doubt to hold us back.

Why is it that we so often fail to act on what we know to be true? The reasons are complex and multifaceted.

One key factor is inertia. We are creatures of habit, and even when our habits don't serve us, they provide a sense of comfort and familiarity. Breaking free from these patterns requires conscious effort and a willingness to step outside our comfort zone, which can be daunting.

Consider the example of Rohan, a talented musician who dreamed of pursuing a career in music. He knew that he needed to dedicate time to practice, network with other musicians, and perform in public to achieve his goal. Yet, he found himself stuck in a cycle of procrastination. He would spend his evenings watching TV, telling himself that he would start tomorrow, or next week, or next month.

Rohan's inertia stemmed from a fear of failure. He worried that he wasn't good enough, that he would be rejected, that he would waste his time and money. This fear, coupled with the comfort of his routine, kept him from taking the necessary steps to pursue his passion.

Another significant obstacle is the "I already know that" syndrome. When we encounter familiar advice, we often dismiss it as being too obvious or simplistic. We assume that because we've heard it before, we've already internalized it and don't need to take any further action. This attitude prevents us from truly engaging with the wisdom and integrating it into our lives.

Think about Priya, who consistently received feedback from her colleagues that she needed to be a more active listener. She acknowledged the feedback, agreeing that it was important, but she didn't make a conscious effort to change her behavior. She believed that because she knew she should listen more, she was already doing it.

Priya's failure to act stemmed from her belief that knowing was enough. She didn't realize that true change requires more than just intellectual understanding; it requires conscious effort, practice, and ongoing self-reflection.

Confronting Inertia and Taking Action

So, how do we overcome these obstacles and bridge the gap between knowing and living? Here are some strategies:

- **Start with small steps:** Overhauling your entire life can feel overwhelming, leading to paralysis. Instead, focus on taking one small, manageable step at a time. If you want to exercise more, start by walking for 10 minutes a day. If you want to improve your relationships, schedule one meaningful conversation with a loved one each week. These small victories build momentum and make larger changes feel less daunting.

- **Make it tangible:** Abstract knowledge is easy to dismiss. Make your goals and intentions concrete by writing them down, creating a visual reminder, or sharing them with someone who will hold you accountable. This transforms your knowledge from a vague idea into a tangible commitment.

- **Embrace discomfort:** Growth happens outside our comfort zone. Be willing to feel uncomfortable, to step into the unknown, and to challenge your привычки. This discomfort is a sign that you are stretching yourself and expanding your horizons.

- **Practice self-compassion:** Changing ingrained patterns takes time and effort. Be patient with yourself, acknowledge your setbacks without judgment, and celebrate your progress, no matter how small. Self-compassion will help you stay motivated and resilient in the face of challenges.

- **Seek support:** You don't have to do it alone. Surround yourself with people who support your goals, encourage your growth, and hold you accountable. Consider working with a coach, joining a support group, or finding a mentor who can guide you on your journey.

- **Focus on the process, not just the outcome:** The pursuit of any meaningful goal will have ups and downs. Instead of fixating solely on the end result, find joy and satisfaction in the process itself. Celebrate the small wins, learn from the setbacks, and appreciate the journey of growth and self-discovery.

The gap between knowing and living is not a chasm but a bridge. It's a bridge we can cross with conscious effort, consistent action, and a willingness to embrace the discomfort of change. By starting small, making our intentions tangible, practicing self-compassion, and seeking support, we can begin to align our lives with our deepest wisdom.

The world is full of people who know what they should do, but are in very short supply are those who do what they know.

Action Plan:

1. Pick one stagnant area (e.g., fitness, relationships). Take a 5-minute daily action (e.g., a stretch routine, a gratitude text).
2. Share a goal with an accountability partner.

Reflection Questions:

1. Where do you feel "stuck" despite knowing what to do?
2. What comfort zone are you afraid to leave?

CHAPTER EIGHT

A Blueprint for Living a Life of Abundance and Authenticity

It's time to redo your portfolio.

We've journeyed through a redefinition of wealth, explored societal misconceptions about success, and examined the delicate balance between ambition and fulfillment. Now, we arrive at the crucial juncture: **How do we integrate these insights into our daily lives?** How do we move beyond the theoretical and begin constructing a life where abundance and authenticity are not lofty ideals but lived realities? This chapter is your blueprint—a practical guide to designing a life that resonates with your deepest values, a life rich in experiences, meaningful connections, and a profound sense of purpose.

The Power of Intention: Crafting Your Personal Manifesto

The first step in charting a new course is to define your destination. This requires a deep dive within, a process of introspection to articulate your core values and aspirations. What truly matters to you? Is it the freedom to express your creativity, the joy of deep connection with loved ones, the thrill of adventure, or the peace of contributing to something larger than yourself? Your answers to these questions form the bedrock of your personal manifesto—a concise statement of your guiding principles.

Consider the example of Priya, a successful entrepreneur who, on the surface, had it all: a thriving business, a beautiful home, and the admiration of her peers. Yet, she felt a nagging sense of dissatisfaction, a feeling that she was on a treadmill, constantly striving for more without a clear sense of why. She decided to take a step back and embark on a journey of self-discovery. Through journaling, meditation, and conversations with mentors, she identified her core values: creativity, connection, and contribution.

Priya crafted the following personal manifesto: "I am committed to living a life that celebrates creativity, fosters deep connections, and contributes meaningfully to the world. I will prioritize experiences that nourish my soul, relationships that enrich my life, and work that makes a positive impact."

This manifesto became her North Star, guiding her decisions and helping her align her actions with her values. When faced with a business opportunity that promised significant financial gain but would require her to compromise her values, she chose to decline, knowing that it would ultimately lead her further away from her desired life.

Your personal manifesto might be different. It could be a simple statement like, "I will prioritize people over profits," or "I will live each day with gratitude and joy." The key is to make it personal, powerful, and easy to recall. Write it down, display it prominently, and use it as a compass to navigate life's choices.

Mindfulness as a Daily Practice: Cultivating Presence and Gratitude

With your personal manifesto as your guide, the next step is to cultivate the daily habits that will bring your vision to life. Mindfulness, the practice of being fully present in the moment, is a powerful tool for aligning your actions with your intentions. It involves paying attention to your thoughts, feelings, and sensations without judgment, allowing you to break free from the cycle of reactivity and make conscious choices.

Imagine starting your day not by rushing into a whirlwind of emails and meetings, but by taking a few moments for quiet reflection. You sit in stillness, focusing on your breath, noticing the sensations in your body, and observing the flow of your thoughts. You set an intention for the day, perhaps to approach each interaction with kindness and compassion, or to fully engage in the task at hand.

Throughout the day, you practice bringing your attention back to the present moment whenever you notice your mind wandering. During a meeting, you listen deeply to what others are saying, rather than formulating your response. While eating lunch, you savor each bite, appreciating the flavors and textures. In the evening, you take a few moments to express gratitude for the day's blessings, no matter how small.

This practice of mindfulness, integrated into your daily routine, transforms the way you experience life. It allows you to appreciate the simple joys, to navigate challenges with greater equanimity, and to cultivate deeper connections with yourself and others.

The Art of Conscious Consumption: Investing in Experiences, Not Just Things

We've discussed how society often equates wealth with material possessions, leading to a relentless pursuit of more. The blueprint for abundance and authenticity involves a conscious shift in how we allocate our resources, prioritizing experiences that enrich our lives over things that merely accumulate dust.

Consider the example of David, a successful lawyer who had spent years working long hours to acquire a collection of luxury cars, designer clothes, and a sprawling mansion. While he enjoyed these possessions, he realized that they provided only fleeting moments of pleasure. He felt a growing sense of emptiness, a longing for something more meaningful.

David decided to experiment with a different approach. He sold one of his luxury cars and used the money to take his family on a trip to Machu Picchu. As they hiked through the ancient ruins, marveling at the breathtaking scenery and learning about the rich history of the Inca civilization, David felt a sense of connection and joy that far surpassed any material possession.

He began to consciously allocate a portion of his income to experiences: taking his children to concerts, learning to play the saxophone, and volunteering at a local soup kitchen. He discovered that these experiences not only brought him greater happiness but also deepened his relationships and gave him a sense of purpose.

Conscious consumption is not about denying yourself all material comforts. It's about making intentional choices about how you spend your money, aligning your spending with your values and priorities. It's about asking yourself, **"Will this purchase truly enhance my life, or will it simply add to the clutter?"**

Nurturing Your Tribe: The Power of Meaningful Connections

No blueprint for abundance and authenticity would be complete without addressing the importance of human connection. Meaningful relationships are the cornerstone of a fulfilling life, providing us with love, support, and a sense of belonging. Yet, in our fast-paced, hyper-connected world, genuine connection can be elusive.

Sarah, a tech executive, realized that while she had hundreds of connections on social media, she lacked true intimacy in her life. She felt lonely and isolated, despite being surrounded by people. She decided to make a conscious effort to cultivate deeper relationships.

Sarah started by reaching out to old friends she had lost touch with, scheduling regular phone calls and get-togethers. She joined a book club, where she met people who shared her interests and engaged in stimulating conversations. She also made a point of being more present and engaged in her interactions with her family and colleagues, listening deeply and expressing her authentic self.

Over time, Sarah's efforts paid off. She developed a close circle of friends who provided her with unwavering support and companionship. She felt more connected to her family and experienced greater joy and fulfillment in her relationships.

Nurturing your tribe requires intentionality and effort. It involves being vulnerable, expressing your needs, and investing time and energy in the people who matter most. It's about creating a community where you feel seen, heard, and loved.

Embracing Impermanence: Finding Joy in the Here and Now

A key aspect of living a life of abundance and authenticity is accepting the impermanent nature of life. Everything changes—our relationships, our circumstances, our own bodies. Resisting this reality leads to suffering, while embracing it allows us to appreciate the preciousness of each moment.

Imagine a beautiful sunset. You watch as the sky transforms into a canvas of vibrant colors, knowing that this breathtaking display will soon fade. Instead of clinging to the moment, trying to hold on to its beauty, you simply allow yourself to be present, to fully experience the wonder of it all.

This is the essence of embracing impermanence: to let go of our attachment to things being a certain way, to accept the ebb and flow of life, and to find joy in the here and now. It's about savoring the present moment, knowing that it is a gift, and appreciating the beauty that surrounds us, even in the midst of change.

The Courage to Be Authentic: Living Your Truth

Authenticity is the foundation of a meaningful life. It's about being true to yourself, expressing your unique gifts and talents, and living in alignment with your values, even when it's difficult or unpopular.

Consider the story of Michael, an artist who had spent years working in a corporate job to please his parents and ensure financial security. He was successful by conventional standards, but he felt a deep sense of unease, a feeling that he was living a lie.

Michael finally decided to listen to his inner voice and pursue his passion for art. It was a scary decision, filled with uncertainty and financial risk. But as he began to create and share his art, he felt a sense of liberation and joy that he had never experienced before.

He faced criticism and doubt from some, but he also attracted a community of people who resonated with his authentic expression. He discovered that living his truth was not only more fulfilling but also more inspiring to others.

The courage to be authentic requires vulnerability and self-acceptance. It involves letting go of the need for external validation and trusting your inner wisdom. It's about embracing your imperfections, celebrating your uniqueness, and living a life that is a true reflection of who you are.

A Continuous Journey: Growth, Evolution, and Adaptation

This blueprint is not a rigid formula but a flexible framework for living. The path to abundance and authenticity is not a destination but a continuous journey of growth, evolution, and adaptation.

As you begin to implement these principles, you will undoubtedly encounter challenges and setbacks. There will be times when you feel lost, confused, or tempted to revert to old patterns. But these moments are not failures; they are opportunities for learning and growth.

The key is to approach life with curiosity, compassion, and a willingness to adapt. Be open to new experiences, embrace change, and continuously refine your blueprint as you evolve. Remember that the goal is not to achieve perfection but to live a life that is constantly becoming more aligned with your values and aspirations.

Designing Your Abundant and Authentic Life

The time to begin is now. Don't wait for the perfect moment or for all the pieces to fall into place. Start with one small step, one conscious choice that aligns with your vision of abundance and authenticity.

Perhaps it's taking a few moments for mindfulness each day, expressing gratitude to someone you appreciate, or scheduling time for an experience that nourishes your soul.

Whatever it is, take that first step with intention and courage. And as you continue on this journey, remember that you are not alone. There is a growing community of people who are committed to living lives of meaning and purpose. Connect with them, share your experiences, and support each other along the way.The world needs your unique gifts, your authentic expression, and your unwavering commitment to living a life that truly matters. Embrace your potential, design your blueprint, and embark on this extraordinary journey of creating a life of abundance and authenticity.tion, and adaptation.

Action Plan:

1. Draft a 3-sentence personal manifesto (e.g., "I prioritize curiosity over comfort").
2. Declutter one space (physical/digital) to reduce distractions from what matters.

Reflection Questions:

1. What does "authenticity" cost you today? What would it gain you?
2. Who in your life embodies the abundance you seek?

CHAPTER NINE

ADDRESSING THE CRITICISMS: THE UNIVERSAL PURSUIT OF AUTHENTIC HAPPINESS

Some have said, *"Amit, you've spent 30 years in the U.S., worked for tech giants, and built an enviable career. Your perspective is privileged. Your advice doesn't apply to us."*

It's true that my experiences have shaped my perspective. I've had the privilege of witnessing firsthand how the relentless pursuit of traditional success—the ambition, the unchecked stress, and the constant chase for more—can erode life's deeper joys.

But to those who say my advice doesn't apply, I offer this: **My experience is not an excuse, but a lens through** which I've observed a universal truth: True wealth is not a substitute for health, meaningful relationships, and a profound sense of purpose.

The insights I've gained from my journey are not about offering a one-size-fits-all blueprint. Rather, they highlight the common threads that weave through all our lives, regardless of background or circumstance. Whether you grew up in middle-class India, navigate the complexities of a corporate career, or have achieved financial stability, we all share a fundamental challenge: the inertia that keeps us from acting on what we know will lead to a more fulfilling life.

Throughout this book, I've challenged the conventional markers of success—those ever-expanding bank balances and property portfolios—and dared to ask a crucial question: What if true wealth lies in the rich tapestry of our experiences, the depth of our relationships, and the quiet moments of self-discovery? This is not a question for the privileged few; it's a question for every human being who has ever felt the nagging sense that there must be more to life than the relentless pursuit of external validation.

The stories shared in these pages—from the reluctant leaps of faith to the transformative epiphanies that arise when we choose to invest in moments over material accumulation—are not meant to be aspirational fantasies. They are intended to serve as mirrors, reflecting your own untapped potential for change and fulfillment. They illustrate the universal struggle to break free from ingrained habits and societal expectations, and the courage it takes to redefine success on our own terms.

I encourage you to look within and ask yourself: Are you truly living the life you envision? Or are you caught in the inertia of habits and expectations passed down through generations? Are you prioritizing what truly nourishes your soul, or are you sacrificing your well-being on the altar of achievement?

The time for introspection is over. Now is the time to act. **Start with a single, bold step.**

Choose to rearrange your priorities, even if it feels as though the wisdom you've always known is too obvious to matter. Perhaps it's planning that long-overdue trip, taking up a new hobby that ignites your passion, or simply dedicating a few precious moments each day to connect with those who matter most. Each small decision, each conscious choice to prioritize well-being and connection over the relentless chase for more, is a seed from which a richer, more meaningful life can grow.

I urge you to lean into the discomfort of change, to embrace the unknown with courage, and to reimagine your path forward. In every decision you make, remember that you have the power to redefine success, not just for yourself, but for those around you. Your journey towards authentic happiness has the potential to transform not only your own life, but also the lives of those you touch.

As I close this book, I invite you to share your journey with others. Whether through conversations with loved ones, personal reflections in a journal, or sharing your insights with a wider audience, let your story inspire others to embark on their own path towards a more fulfilling life. Your insights, your struggles, and your triumphs have the power to spark change far beyond your immediate circle.

Remember, the path to a truly fulfilling life is rarely linear. It's a winding road filled with both challenges and opportunities for growth. Every step you take, no matter how small, adds to the rich and vibrant mosaic of your legacy. So, carry these lessons with you, be the change you wish to see in the world, and embrace the power of investing in happiness.

With heartfelt gratitude and hope, let's keep the coversation going.

Amit Chopra

Stay in touch !

https://www.linkedin.com/in/amitchopra/
www.chopra.dev

Appendix

Key Takeaways:

- Define your core values and aspirations to create a personal manifesto.
- Cultivate mindfulness as a daily practice to enhance presence and gratitude.
- Practice conscious consumption, prioritizing experiences over material possessions.
- Nurture meaningful connections with a supportive community.
- Embrace impermanence and find joy in the present moment.
- Have the courage to live authentically, expressing your unique truth.
- View life as a continuous journey of growth, evolution, and adaptation.

Resources for readers:

- **Books**: Die With Zero (Bill Perkins), Ikigai (Héctor García).
- **Podcasts**: On Purpose with Jay Shetty, The Happiness Lab.
- **Indian Communities:** The Minimalist Indian, MentorTogether.

www.ingramcontent.com/pod-product-compliance
Lightning Source LLC
Chambersburg PA
CBHW020506160726
47991CB00007B/2831